GLOBAL ORGANIZATIONS

UNICEF

Sean Connolly

Smart Apple Media

Smart Apple Media is published by Black Rabbit Books
P.O. Box 3263, Mankato, Minnesota 56002

Printed in Hong Kong

Library of Congress Cataloging-in-Publication Data

Connolly, Sean, 1956–
    UNICEF / Sean Connolly.
    p. cm.–(Smart apple media. Global organizations)
    Summary: "Describes the efforts of the United Nations Children's Fund
(UNICEF) to help the world's children by increasing their standards of living,
protecting children's rights, and delivering emergency aid"–Provided by publisher.
    Includes index.
    ISBN 978-1-59920-303-4
    1. UNICEF–Juvenile literature. I. Title.
HV703.C66 2009
362.7–dc22

                                                                2007038993

Designed by Helen James
Edited by Mary-jane Wilkins
Picture research by Su Alexander

Photograph acknowledgements
page 6 Giacomo Pirozzi/UNICEF; 9 UNICEF; 11 William Kaufman/UNICEF;
12 UNICEF; 14 Giacomo Pirozzi/UNICEF; 17 Christopher Grant/UNICEF;
18 Susan Markisz/UNICEF; 20 & 22 Josh Estey/UNICEF; 23 Asad Zaidi/UNICEF;
24 & 27 Christine Nesbitt/UNICEF; 28 Dan Thomas/UNICEF; 29 Shehzad
Noorani/UNICEF; 30 Niclas Ryberg/UNICEF; 31 Tom Pietrasik/UNICEF;
34 UNICEF; 36 Bruno Brioni/UNICEF; 38 Susan Markisz/UNICEF;
39 Giacomo Pirozzi/UNICEF; 40 UNICEF; 42 Susan Markisz/UNICEF
Front cover UNICEF

CONTENTS

Giving Children a Chance

If the world were a fairer place, everyone would have the same chances in life. Most children develop into healthy adults if they are given proper medical care, a good education, decent housing, and enough food. What they do after that—choosing a job or deciding where to live and whether to get married—is up to them.

Today, these essential ingredients for healthy development are beyond the reach of many millions of young people. Some parts of the world are in the grip of violence or famine; people in other countries face terrible diseases or are threatened by natural disasters.

Children play in the new playground at a school in southern Pakistan. UNICEF provided educational materials, playground equipment, and health materials for the school, as well as a teacher-training program.

International Recognition

In 1965, UNICEF was awarded one of the highest honors in the world—the Nobel Peace Prize. This annual award recognizes contributions made by organizations and individuals in the cause of world peace. The 1965 award noted UNICEF's tireless efforts to improve living conditions for the world's children. UNICEF was also linked to the 2006 Nobel Peace Prize. That year's winner, Muhammad Yunus, has linked his Grameen Bank with UNICEF to lend money to poor people in Bangladesh. The money is lent mainly to women in order to create jobs and fight poverty.

The United Nations Children's Fund (UNICEF) was founded in 1946 with the aim of giving all children a chance to start their lives with the same basic rights. Since then, the world's population has increased by more than four billion. This rise puts a strain on food supplies and makes it harder for people in developing countries to live comfortably. Violence and disease continue to threaten children everywhere. But despite these problems, UNICEF has led the world in improving life for the world's children.

Solid Success

In the 60 years since UNICEF was founded, it has contributed enormously to the standard of living that children experience around the world. The following four key improvements, quoted on the UNICEF Web site, clearly demonstrate some remarkable successes:

- A generation ago, 70,000 children died every day. Today, that number has been cut by more than half.
- Thirty years ago, one in four children died before the age of five. Today, that number is less than one in ten.
- In 1980, ten percent of the world's children were immunized against six killer diseases. Today, that number is over 75 percent.
- This year, three million more children will live to their fifth birthday than in 1990, and tens of millions will lead healthier, more productive lives than they would have done previously.

Wars and Peace

By 1945, there had been two world wars in just over 30 years. Sixty million people died during World War II, and more than half were civilians. Millions more were left homeless, especially in Europe, which was the main battleground from 1939 to 1945.

Just weeks after the war ended in Europe—and while the war continued in Asia—world leaders gathered in San Francisco to establish a new organization. Its name was the United Nations (UN), and it aimed to build peace after the war. World War II had ended by the time the UN came into being on October 24, 1945.

Loss and Rebuilding

The UN began in a world shattered by war. As well as the millions of dead and displaced people, much of Europe had been flattened in the fighting. Parts of many great cities lay in ruins; roads and railways were destroyed; hospitals and schools were damaged or destroyed.

The people who suffered most as a result of all this were children. The UN and other international organizations saw that millions of children, especially in Europe, needed better medical care, education, housing, and clothing. In 1946, the United Nations International Children's Emergency Fund (UNICEF) was formed to help children affected by the war. At that stage, it was a temporary organization that was expected to close when its job was done.

A Permanent Mission

UNICEF proved to be so good at its job that the United Nations made it a permanent organization in 1953. It shortened its name to the United Nations Children's Fund, but kept the abbreviation UNICEF because it is easier to say. The organization immediately began to tackle international issues. In 1953, it began a successful

Germany, 1946: a young girl —one of millions of Europeans left homeless by World War II—sits wrapped in blankets on a pile of belongings.

campaign against a disease called yaws, helping millions of children worldwide to receive penicillin that treated the disease.

At the same time, UNICEF began programs to improve education, housing, and living conditions for the world's children. It was given an enormous boost when Danny Kaye, one of the most popular film stars of the time, volunteered to become UNICEF's ambassador at large. This high-profile involvement helped to publicize the work of UNICEF, and it started a tradition of appointing goodwill ambassadors, a practice which other international organizations have followed.

*Opposite page
Hollywood film star Danny Kaye amuses a group of children in a Thai village during the filming of* Assignment: Children. *The film, and Kaye's enthusiastic involvement, helped to publicize UNICEF and its work around the world.*

UNICEF's Aims

The organization's aims are as follows:

- Children have rights
- The world has set goals for children
- Children demand a voice
- Poverty reduction starts with children
- The people of the world say "Yes" for children
- Children should not be dying from preventable diseases

Eglantyne Jebb

UNICEF was not the first organization to focus on the needs of children around the world. In 1919, not long after the end of World War I, a British woman named Eglantyne Jebb founded the Save the Children Fund. Like UNICEF, Webb's organization aimed to improve living conditions for German and Austrian children. Jebb worked tirelessly to make life better for the world's children, and to provide guidelines to protect children's rights. In 1923, she wrote the *Declaration of the Rights of the Child*. More than 30 years later, the United Nations expanded this document to produce its own *Declaration of the Rights of the Child*. In 1989, the UN took things a step further with its Convention on the Rights of the Child. Since then, UNICEF has worked to put these UN statements into practice around the world.

... ON THE SCENE ... ON THE SCENE ... ON THE SCENE ...

Lasting Link

In 1953, film star Danny Kaye was on a flight from London to New York when one of the plane's engines caught fire. The plane landed safely in Ireland and Kaye was able continue his journey. For the rest of the long flight, he sat next to Maurice Pate, who was the first executive director of UNICEF. Pate explained that one of UNICEF's main problems was that few people had heard of it.

The film star agreed to help by visiting a number of UNICEF projects in Asia. The result was a film called Assignment: Children, *which was seen by more than 100 million people. Kaye insisted that the film's profits went to UNICEF. It was the beginning of a link with UNICEF that lasted until he died in 1987. Near the end of his life he said, "I feel that the most rewarding thing I have ever done in my life is to be associated with UNICEF."*

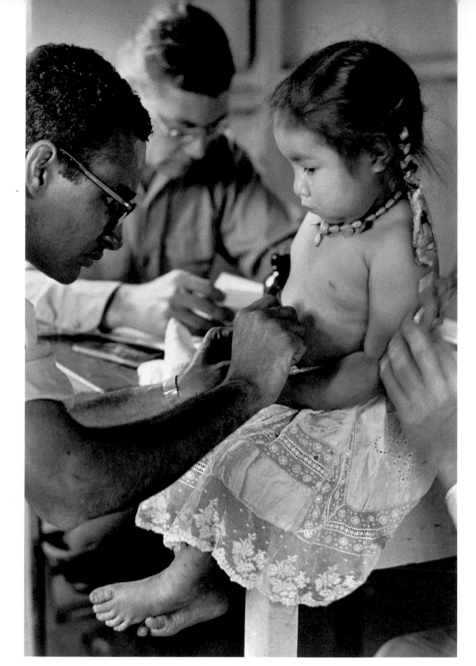

A medical worker examines a young Native American girl at a health center in Amatitlan, Guatemala. UNICEF has helped to fund care and training programs for health centers in rural Guatemala.

These aims tie UNICEF neatly into the wider United Nations community. Other UN agencies focus on a close range of issues. The World Health Organization (WHO), as its name suggests, tackles problems of disease and health. The United Nations Educational, Scientific, and Cultural Organization (UNESCO) identifies education as a tool for progress. The Food and Agriculture Organization (FAO) aims to help even the poorest countries produce enough food to feed their people.

UNICEF, however, considers all of these subjects to be part of its mission. It also adds another important element to the equation —time. By focusing on children, UNICEF is helping to build a better world for the future.

Tradition and Progress

Like any organization, UNICEF has had to change with the times. New threats—for example, natural disasters such as the 2004 tsunami or health crises such as HIV/AIDS—appear from nowhere. UNICEF must be able to react quickly and efficiently, just as it must be aware of the latest tools to help with its job.

The main aim of UNICEF—helping children—remains the same as more than 60 years ago. The ways in which the organization can help children, and the ways in which their needs are identified, are part of the twenty-first century. UNICEF now sees itself as a vital part of the United Nations Millennium Development Goals (see pages 36–37). As a result, it groups its activities in five strategic areas that tie in with UN goals.

Young Child Survival and Development

Children's first month—and the months before they are born—often determine their health in later life. UNICEF promotes basic medical care for all children. In the meantime, it provides essential vaccines for 40 percent of children in the poorest countries. It also works with governments and other organizations to deliver medicines to the neediest.

Basic Education and Gender Equality

In addition to providing schools with equipment, UNICEF aims to include children who might otherwise be denied education, such as the poorest children, or girls. It also offers emergency schools and advises governments on action.

HIV/AIDS

UNICEF links up with governments and organizations to fight and educate people about this deadly disease, which particularly affects Africa and other developing parts of the world.

Flying Start

During its first five years (while it was still a temporary organization), UNICEF spent $115 million on:
- distributing clothes to five million children in 12 countries;
- vaccinating eight million children against tuberculosis;
- rebuilding milk distribution networks across Europe; and
- providing an extra meal to millions of needy children every day.

Child Protection

UNICEF helps to enforce laws that protect the rights of children. These might be laws against poor working conditions or laws that aim to stop children from being forced to become soldiers. UNICEF also acts as a watchdog, observing governments in countries where it operates and helping to ensure that they enforce these laws.

Partnerships for Children's Rights

UNICEF has a long tradition of teaming up with governments, organizations, companies, and individuals to ensure that children's needs come first. It also conducts a great deal of research on conditions worldwide. The results of this research help the UN and other organizations to keep track of human rights.

A girl practices handwriting in a UNICEF-funded school in Pakistan. These school programs aim to increase standards of literacy as well as health.

Framework for Help

As a United Nations organization, UNICEF reflects the wishes and policies of the General Assembly. The organization chooses the best ways of working, but its mission statement outlines its aims.

UNICEF's mission statement states that it should:
- advocate for the protection of children's rights;
- help meet their basic needs; and
- expand their opportunities to reach their full potential.

To meet these aims, the organization needs a structure. Like the UN, UNICEF is based in New York. The UN General Assembly decides on the overall strategy that UNICEF should adopt. It gives guidance —for example, strengthening UNICEF's role in supporting children's rights—but it does not insist on doing the same things in the same way in every country. UNICEF has an executive director, whose job is like that of a president or prime minister of a country. The executive director offers leadership and direction. A 36-member executive board (elected by the UN) and UNICEF's eight regional offices help in this process.

Meeting the People

The core work of UNICEF is in the field, working in 156 countries where the organization has a presence. This work is carried out in 126 country offices (some of which serve several countries). A UNICEF country office works with that country's government to plan activities. These are projects involving UNICEF that are part of a five-year program that helps women and children in the most practical ways.

Most of the 10,000 people who work for UNICEF are field workers. They transport medicine, set up schools and medical clinics, distribute food, and check on children's rights. These workers also report back to headquarters through country and regional offices, in order to help worldwide planning.

*Opposite page
A Danish worker packs UNICEF schools-in-a-box (see page 26) to send to New Orleans in September 2005. UNICEF's central warehouse in Copenhagen sent 235 schools-in-a-box and 740 recreation kits for children displaced by Hurricane Katrina.*

... ON THE SCENE ... ON THE SCENE ... ON THE SCENE ...

The Long Way Round

From April to July 2004, film star Ewan McGregor and his friend Charlie Boorman traveled by motorcycle from London to New York—going east. The 18,887-mile (30,395-km) trip was to publicize UNICEF. (McGregor had become a goodwill ambassador that year). A film crew followed the pair. The journey became a film, TV series, and book, all with the title The Long Way Round. *Viewers could see McGregor and Boorman stopping at UNICEF projects in Russia, Ukraine, Kazakhstan, and Mongolia.*

The project inspired others to follow in the tracks of McGregor and Boorman and to support UNICEF in the process. In July 2006, a group of 19 bikers from Yorkshire, England, set off on a 3,480-mile (5,600-km) journey from London to Ukraine, raising money for UNICEF projects there. Boorman met them in London, saying, "It's an honor to think that The Long Way Round *has inspired others to raise money to support the incredible work that UNICEF is doing for the children of Kiev."*

Mixed Blessing

Many non-governmental organizations (NGOs), such as the International Red Cross and Oxfam, have no ties to any government. UNICEF is different. In many ways it is a team made up of representatives of many governments. This difference is important. Because of the government connection, UNICEF can sometimes take action more quickly and efficiently. Its goods can be carried on government vehicles and stored in warehouses guarded by police or soldiers. This cooperation can extend to a local level as well, so that UNICEF officials can use village halls, local hospitals, and schools.

However, having ties with governments can limit freedom in some ways. Other NGOs find it easier to criticize the actions of governments. UNICEF people need to be more cautious and choose their words carefully. UNICEF has been criticized for not taking a stronger stand against, for example, child slavery in southern Sudan or the issue of child soldiers in Western Africa.

Who Pays for It All?

Although UNICEF is part of the United Nations, it receives no money from the UN. Instead, the organization receives $3 billion a year from national governments, individuals, and companies, and from the 38 UNICEF national committees. These committees, based in the world's richest countries, help plan activities and raise money. Some committees make larger contributions to UNICEF than their country's government. Two-thirds of funds come from national governments. These funds are separate from contributions to the UN itself. Some governments specify how they would like the money spent. For example, in December 2006, the Dutch government gave $201 billion to provide schools and equipment for areas hit by conflict or natural disaster.

A banner promoting children's rights hangs from a street lamp outside the United Nations Headquarters in May 2002. The UN Special Session on Children was held from May 8-10, 2002.

Reporting to the World

Imagine what it must be like to have a plane full of blankets, medicine, powdered milk, and bottled water. You need to deliver these goods to earthquake victims quickly, but you don't know which airport is closest to the earthquake zone—or whether it is big enough for your plane to land.

Or, maybe your government wants you to spend millions of dollars to help starving people in Africa. You know that many people are suffering, but you don't want to waste time and money finding them.

UNICEF can help in cases like these. It can pass on some of the knowledge and experience it has gained from the special way it works. Many of its projects last for years, giving UNICEF the chance to get to know a country very well. This knowledge can save many lives in times of emergency.

Inside Stories

This knowledge and experience helps UNICEF publicize many issues —children being forced to become soldiers, unexploded land mines and their dangers, dangerous working practices, and much more.

UNICEF is widely respected for three publications in particular. *The State of the World's Children*, published every year, is the most detailed study of children in the world. It combines human stories with maps and studies, highlighting some of the 195 countries and

UNICEF joined forces with other agencies after the Indian Ocean tsunami in December 2004. These Indonesian workers are unloading emergency supplies sent by UNICEF and the European Commission Humanitarian Office (ECHO).

territories that it covers. *Progress for Children* has been published two or three times a year since 2004. It reads somewhat like a school report and offers updates on progress towards the Millennium Development Goals (see pages 36–37). The *UNICEF Annual Report* focuses on the progress UNICEF and its partners have made for children each year.

... ON THE SCENE ... ON THE SCENE ... ON THE SCENE ...

Camel Jockeys

Camel racing is a popular sport in parts of the Middle East. Camel owners often use children as jockeys because they are light, which gives the camel a better chance of winning. But apart from being young (some are only five years old), many of the jockeys do not come from the country where they race. They are taken from their home countries (usually Pakistan or India) and have to work in difficult conditions.

UNICEF has investigated the problem of underage camel jockeys for years, reporting its findings to the wider world and working for change in countries where camel racing takes place. In June 2005, UNICEF signed an agreement with the United Arab Emirates (UAE) to end the practice. The UAE banned children from being jockeys if they are under age 16, or weigh less than 100 pounds (45 kg).

Then the UAE began sending child jockeys back to their families. Among a group of 22 who arrived back in Pakistan on June 21, 2005 was 15-year-old Ghulam Sarwar. He had spent half of his life as a camel jockey. In return, his family received a small fee and he was paid a few dollars a month.

"Sometimes I had enough to eat, and sometimes not. They would hit us when we made mistakes," Ghulam recalled. "The job is very tiresome. We had to work from morning to night, tenting the camels, training them, cleaning their waste, and racing in the games. I was lonely. I missed my parents. I didn't like it there at all, but I had no way out."

Thanks to the hard work of UNICEF, Ghulam and other young camel jockeys have found a way out.

Helping the UN

United Nations agencies have developed in a way that promotes cooperation among them. One important area of cooperation is ensuring that some tasks, both routine and special, are not duplicated.

Supplies of clean water were cut off in many areas hit by the 2004 tsunami. UNICEF supplied six of the 65 water trucks for Lampeuneurut, a region in the Indonesian province of Aceh.

For example, it would be a huge waste of UN money if representatives of several agencies arrived at the scene of an earthquake at the same time and each started to write a report about the damage. It makes much more sense to give one agency the job of making the first on-the-spot decisions. In that way, representatives of agencies will have inside knowledge of what is needed before they arrive. Without that coordination, too many blankets and tents might be supplied, for example, and not enough bandages or fresh water.

UNICEF has a special role in UN emergency action. The United Nations has given it the responsibility to act as cluster leader in data communications during emergencies. UNICEF took on this role many times during the Indian Ocean tsunami of 2004 and after the severe earthquake in Pakistan in 2005.

UNICEF is the ideal choice to be the front-line decision-maker in emergencies around the world. In the case of the 2005 earthquake, it had operated within Pakistan—in many different roles—since the country's founding in 1947. UNICEF teams had helped local people through a number of natural disasters and knew exactly where and how to mobilize relief efforts. This experience, coupled with the contacts developed with government departments, meant the agency could offer guidance to other aid agencies.

Pakistani children head home with UNICEF emergency kits of warm clothing and other winter essentials. A powerful earthquake in 2005 affected much of the country, leaving millions of people desperate for help during the bitter winter high up in the mountains.

The Thick of Things

The Kounoungo refugee camp in

the African country of Chad is not a pretty place. Only a few scrub trees, shrubs, and the occasional large rock break the monotony of the dry, dusty landscape. But to the thousands of Sudanese people who now live there, Kounoungo is a place of safety and hope.

UNICEF is part of the reason these people feel hopeful. More than 100,000 of them (two-thirds of them children) have crossed the border from Sudan into Chad. These people were forced from their homes in the Sudanese region of Darfur by the fierce fighting that has

Sometimes a little help can go a long way. These boys are playing a spirited match in a center for Sudanese refugees in eastern Chad (UNICEF provided the soccer ball). The organization also arranged for teacher training and essential school materials for the refugee camp.

continued for more than three years. The fighting destroyed farms and made the countryside unsafe for villagers, even if they could grow their own food.

UNICEF has helped to set up schools in Kounoungo and other refugee camps along Chad's eastern border with Sudan. The school in Kounoungo is a simple, wood-frame building with plastic sheeting for a roof and walls. Inside, more than 1,700 children crowd together for lessons. No one seems to mind sitting on the dirt floor for hours on end. The young Sudanese children have notebooks, pencils, and rulers supplied by UNICEF, which also helps to train teachers from among the older refugees. The children are eager to learn and eager to return to the part of their childhood that has not been taken away by the fighting.

Basic Needs

Many UNICEF operations, such as the one in Kounoungo, are in the front line of violence and crisis. Inevitably, children suffer during conflicts and war. Apart from the obvious risks to their health and their lives, they often do not have fresh water, food, schooling, health care, and many other basic needs of childhood. UNICEF identifies four key areas in which help is needed during an emergency, whether the emergency is natural or man-made (see pages 26–29).

ON THE SCENE ... ON THE SCENE ... ON THE SCENE ...

Chekhadine Adam Ibrahim, age 10, describes his life as a refugee in Chad: *"We had to flee because the Janjaweed [gunmen supported by the Sudanese government] came to attack our village. They burned the houses and also the shops. I saw my house burning. We had to flee into the bush with my mom and my four brothers. My father stayed in Bensaliba. At school, the lessons are interesting. I would like to become a teacher."*

School-in-a-Box

UNICEF has been concerned with education throughout its history. Its connection with learning covers all areas, from providing pencils and paper to children in a flooded village, to helping countries decide how to spend their money over the next five years. Education has many benefits. The obvious one is training young people to use their abilities and skills fully in later life. Returning to school after an interruption because of a natural disaster or conflict is very important if children are to build on their learning.

A return to school has other, less obvious, benefits. Returning to daily routines, such as going to school, can help children recover psychologically from terrible shocks. To help the hundreds of thousands of Rwandan refugees in 1994, UNICEF developed special school-in-a-box kits. The organization had decades of experience of supplying pre-packed boxes of food and medicine. They used the same thinking to produce kits that could be used in a makeshift classroom.

Every school-in-a-box arrives in an aluminum box. Teachers can paint the lid of the box and use it as a blackboard. Inside is basic equipment for pupils: pencils, paper, scissors, and erasers, as well as a teaching clock, counting cubes, and posters to help the children with alphabet and number skills.

The purpose of the kit is to allow education to continue during the first 72 hours of an emergency, a time that is especially important for children. UNICEF also distributes recreation kits, because sports and play are also important for children during an emergency. Every kit has jerseys, whistles, balls, and scoring slates that allow up to 40 children to play.

1 Health and Nutrition

UNICEF helps to distribute basic medicine and drugs to fight disease and infection. It provides equipment for medical clinics, warm blankets and clothes, and easy-to-distribute emergency food supplies.

2 Education

The organization helps to make sure that children have safe places for learning and play. UNICEF also trains teachers and provides basic school supplies.

Opposite page
A Liberian girl in a camp for displaced persons learns the alphabet from the lid of a school-in-a-box. These portable educational kits help children to continue learning despite some enormous obstacles.

After the Tsunami

The tsunami that swept across the Indian Ocean on December 26, 2004 killed 230,000 people and left millions without houses, schools, food supplies, or medical care. UNICEF responded fast and began emergency and long-term rebuilding programs across the region. A report written two years after the tsunami estimates that UNICEF reached 4.8 million children and women in eight countries. One of the biggest tasks is replacing damaged or destroyed schools.

One of UNICEF's success stories was in the village of Kampong Baro, in the Indonesian province of Aceh (which was hit first and hardest by the tsunami). Kampong Baro's new school was one of 36 that UNICEF completed in the region by late 2006. This was not a return to the way things were before the tsunami, but ten-year-old Mouri was very pleased with the new school: "The old school was always flooded. It was not comfortable. It wasn't good for studying. The new school is comfortable, and it's not noisy."

3 Child Protection

This role is important during a crisis, when children are often separated from their families. UNICEF provides care and counseling and teaches children how to avoid land mines and live wires.

4 Water Supply and Sanitation

This basic need can become the foundation for all other relief work in a disaster zone. Without fresh water, children are in danger

Signs warn of land mines in western Cambodia, one of the most heavily mined areas in the world. Land mines kill children years after wars end.

Girls collect fresh water from a UNICEF-supplied tank at a camp for displaced people in northeastern Sri Lanka. The label on the tank also gives advice on basic hygiene.

of dehydration. UNICEF also helps to ensure that there is water to help waste drain away fast. Fatal diseases can quickly spread through a disaster area without a working water supply.

UNICEF is often the first outside group to arrive at the scene of an emergency and the last one to leave. With its thousands of field workers in 155 countries—most of them able to call on the help of local governments—it has an advantage in reaching an emergency. And because UNICEF has broader responsibilities than just emergencies—responsibilities tied in with childhood itself—it stays to make sure that children resume some sort of normal life.

... ON THE SCENE ... ON THE SCENE ... ON THE SCENE ...

Earthquake Relief

A powerful earthquake hit Pakistan on October 8, 2005. Thousands of people were killed or left homeless, and there was a desperate shortage of medicine and food. To make matters worse, winter was fast approaching in this mountainous region. UNICEF helped from the first day by sending trucks of supplies to the earthquake zone. Helicopters took supplies to remote villages and returned with injured children. Meanwhile, UNICEF cargo planes from Copenhagen flew to Pakistan with more supplies. UNICEF workers on the scene helped to check on the health and safety of the homeless people living in temporary shelters. Education Officer Khalida Ahmad helped to prevent an outbreak of disease by monitoring the quality of the water supply: "We see people washing clothes and drinking water and the water is mixed."

A man holds his young son, who has been treated at a temporary medical clinic for people displaced by the 2005 earthquake in Pakistan.

A Team Player

The UNICEF Web site says: "We have the global authority to influence decision-makers, and the variety of partners at grassroots level to turn the most innovative ideas into reality."

This single sentence helps to explain some of the special qualities of UNICEF and why it is both successful and essential to the modern world. The sentence says much more than seems apparent at first. Having global authority, for example, means a great deal when you are trying to persuade a government to change its ways. The decision-makers UNICEF seeks to influence are in a position to make the

Roger Federer, UNICEF goodwill ambassador and tennis star, visited several tsunami-recovery programs in southern India during December 2006.

... ON THE SCENE ... ON THE SCENE ... ON THE SCENE ...

A Champion's Visit

Tennis star Roger Federer has been a goodwill ambassador since April 2006. His connection with UNICEF goes back to March 11, 2005, when he organized the ATP All-Star Rally for Relief. That tennis event supported UNICEF after the 2004 tsunami.

In December 2006, Federer visited Cuddalore, in southern India, to see how people are coping two years after the tsunami. When asked why he had chosen to become involved, Federer said, "I would rather step in early than late. I am in the prime of my career. I am making so much money and I realize how lucky I have been."

This was Federer's first trip to India, and he visited an orphanage, an education center, and an HIV awareness unit. UNICEF has played a part in all of them. Federer understood how he can help both locally and internationally: "Kids are the future. I inspire them and in turn they inspire me. I have made some really good friends here today. I spent quite some time with the children. I know what their names are and what they study," he said.

"I am happy to see happy faces in all the kids here... both young and old. It's nice to see that a great program is happening here. You can be proud of the government and the people and UNICEF who have helped in this."

necessary changes. Partners at grassroots level can mean anyone from interested individuals to powerful local companies—both know far more about what is going on than an outsider. Anyone can come up with innovative ideas, but it takes real skill and dedication to make them work.

This all adds up to clever ideas about teamwork and partnership. UNICEF has an advantage over many international organizations in these two areas, and it is constantly finding new ways to make the most of this advantage.

Partners with Business

UNICEF has a tradition of working with partners in the private sector. Businesses, ranging from tiny family-run firms to large corporations, are welcome to play a part in the programs that UNICEF devises and oversees.

Goodwill Ambassadors

What do David Beckham, Jackie Chan, Roger Federer, and Whoopi Goldberg have in common? Apart from the fact that each is well known in his or her field, they have all been goodwill ambassadors for UNICEF. The organization has always welcomed well-known people who can spread the message about its work around the world.

Not every ambassador is expected to travel as much as the first, Danny Kaye (see page 11), who devoted much of his time over 33 years to UNICEF. Some ambassadors, such as Kaye, are ambassadors at large with an international range. Others are regional or national ambassadors, depending on how well known they are and how much time they can spend with UNICEF.

The organization identifies four main ways in which businesses can take on that role:

- by forming creative partnerships;
- by donating funds for UNICEF to administer;
- by donating money to help with an existing UNICEF program; or
- by supporting UNICEF sponsorship schemes within their own work force.

The list of companies that have teamed up with UNICEF is long, ranging from the Aaron Basha jewelry maker to the German Internet company web.de. It includes international computer companies, national airlines, ice cream makers, banks, and major newspapers. All of these companies benefit from their association with UNICEF, while at the same time finding ways to contribute and improve children's lives. More importantly, UNICEF benefits from the different types of experience that each of these companies can offer.

WHAT DO YOU THINK?

Are Business Partnerships OK?
Some people object to international organizations such as UNICEF linking themselves to private companies. They say that the companies are only involved to make money for themselves and that UNICEF loses some of its independence in the process. What do you think?

Closer to Home

Is there a role for UNICEF to play in richer countries, apart from raising money for its work in other parts of the world? There is, even though fundraising remains important.

In remote parts of Central Australia, for example, UNICEF has worked with indigenous young Australians to improve their nutrition, educational opportunities, and overall rights. UNICEF's baby friendly initiative in the UK helps mothers learn more about infant nutrition.

Children at North Nibley Primary School in Gloucestershire, England, dressed in international costumes to raise money on UNICEF Day for Change in 2006.

UNICEF Day for Change

Every year, children in British schools have a chance to raise vital funds for UNICEF while having a lot of fun in the process. A date is chosen as the UNICEF Day for Change. The most recent was February 2, 2007. Schools register to take part and receive an education pack with posters, CDs, PowerPoint presentations, and other materials to make learning fun.

On the Day for Change, schools raise money in unusual ways—dressing up oddly, dressing in national flags, wearing silly hats, or dressing in any other way to draw attention to UNICEF's international work. Registered schools are eligible for a drawing; the 2007 prize sent two pupils and a teacher from two seperate schools to visit UNICEF's supply division in Copenhagen.

Seeing these programs in action shows people the good that UNICEF can do, especially in poorer countries that lack the resources of countries such as Australia or the UK. So the work has an extra benefit beyond the help it gives people in the community.

... ON THE SCENE ... ON THE SCENE ... ON THE SCENE ...

Courageous Mothers

UNICEF Ireland organized a Mother's Day Lunch in Dublin on March 24, 2006. The event raised nearly $53,500 for its Safe Motherhood campaign. All the money went to the campaign, which funds UNICEF programs that aim to prevent the transmission of HIV from mothers to their children throughout Africa.

The special guest at the lunch was film actor Gabriel Byrne, who is a UNICEF Ireland ambassador. Byrne had just finished making a film in the tiny southern African kingdom of Swaziland, where nearly four people in ten carry the HIV virus. He praised the courage of mothers there who were tested to see whether they carried the virus.

Thanks to the medicines available at Safe Motherhood clinics, many newborn babies can now develop without HIV. As Byrne noted: "Without treatment, half of these children die before they reach their second birthday."

Looking Ahead

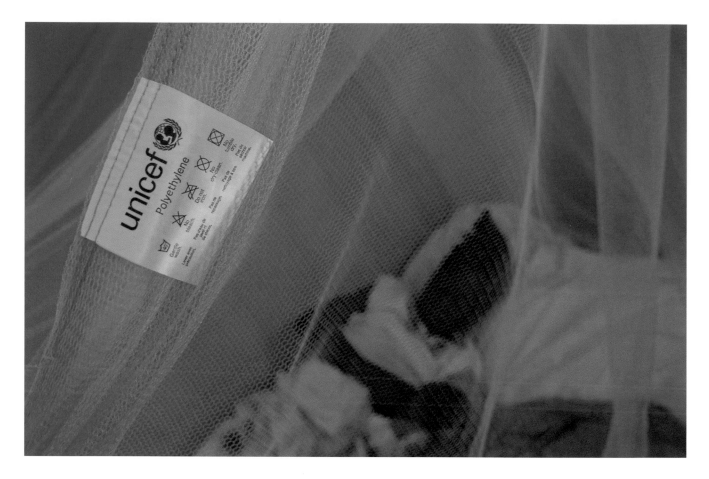

In September 2000, representatives from 189 countries (every UN member country at the time) met to discuss ways of improving life in the new millennium. After a great deal of talk and argument, they came up with eight targets to be achieved by 2015.

These targets, known as Millennium Development Goals (MDGs), are

- To eradicate extreme poverty and hunger
- To achieve universal primary education
- To promote gender equality and empower women
- To reduce child mortality
- To improve maternal health

A mother and her newborn son in Cote d'Ivoire rest under a net supplied by UNICEF and the Japanese government. Bed nets protect people from mosquitoes, which carry malaria. UNICEF also supports other anti-malaria projects in tropical countries.

- To combat HIV/AIDS, malaria, and other diseases
- To ensure environmental sustainability
- To develop a global partnership for development

The first six of these goals are linked directly to children, and children (the leaders of the future) will benefit from the other two. As a result, the MDGs are an important part of UNICEF planning.

Two years later, the United Nations held a Special Session on Children. This three-day meeting of the general assembly was devoted to the needs of young people. It resulted in a list of 21 goals and targets, which covered areas such as medicine, education, and mental health.

The Scale of the Job

Despite the progress it has made in its first 60 years, UNICEF faces some enormous obstacles as it works to meet its MDGs. Below are some of the challenges it has identified.

Child Survival
UNICEF believes that young child survival and development are crucial—the first basic right of any child. Yet more than ten million children under the age of five die every year. Two-thirds of these deaths are preventable.

HIV/AIDS – Care and Support
More than 15 million children have lost one or both parents to AIDS—12 million are in sub-Saharan Africa. By 2010, this number is expected to rise to more than 16 million. UNICEF's challenge is to help the 90 percent of AIDS orphans who receive no support from outside their communities.

Education
To achieve universal primary education by 2015, the number of children enrolling in school worldwide must increase by 1.3 percent each year. This figure is an average, which means some countries need a smaller increase. Other countries have fewer children than average in primary education, so their increase needs to be higher than the average. The small east African country of Eritrea needs to increase numbers of children in primary education by more than 4 percent every year, and Afghanistan's target is only slightly lower.

how does AIDS take a child's life?

UNITE FOR CHILDREN
UNITE AGAINST AIDS

Rights or Survival?

UNICEF began as a temporary organization with a mission to improve conditions for the millions of children whose lives had been shattered by World War II. It fed and clothed many of those children, while making sure they would benefit from health care, education, and housing in the future. The fact that UNICEF continues to exist is a tribute to how well it did its job.

Not long after becoming a permanent UN organization, UNICEF altered its role slightly. Following the lead of the UN, it began to concentrate on children's rights (to protection, health care, shelter, and education). A UN Declaration in 1959 was followed 30 years later by the Convention on the Rights of the Child, which strengthened the earlier document.

It looked as though UNICEF's work would be made easier. After all, many of its aims and targets were now considered rights.

Some people believe that the opposite has happened, and that concentrating on rights has made UNICEF less able to help with food, medicine, and other original targets. Critics believe that UNICEF is now concentrating on politics and not on child survival. A critical article in the British medical journal *The Lancet* in 2004 suggested that the United Nations—and especially UNICEF—could fall short of meeting the MDGs on child health. People continue to argue over this, and only the next few years will tell whether UNICEF has managed to combine its goals for rights with its health targets.

WHAT DO YOU THINK?

How Many Goals?

Do you think that UNICEF can concentrate on improving children's rights while continuing to work for better health and medical treatment for children? Or do you believe that it can really only do one of these jobs well?

*Opposite page
UNICEF's AIDS-awareness messages on the walls of the UN headquarters in October 2005.*

A grandmother in eastern Zimbabwe, whose grandchildren have been orphaned by AIDS, watches them play.

Together these should lead to three main outcomes:
• the best possible start in life for children;
• a good-quality basic education for all children; and
• the opportunity for all children, especially teenagers, for meaningful participation in their communities.

The UN gave itself ten years, until 2012, to achieve these children's targets, and UNICEF is playing a major part in the process.

Young Voices

Children and young people have been captivated by UNICEF's work for more than six decades. It is hardly surprising that the young take a real interest in an organization devoted to young people.

This interest blossoms in many ways: raising money at Halloween, representing UNICEF in Model United Nations days, or simply reading up on the organization's work around the world and considering how to help.

These young supporters are playing an active part in the UNICEF campaign to Make Poverty History.

... ON THE SCENE ... ON THE SCENE ... ON THE SCENE ...

A Family Commitment

Film actress Mia Farrow has been a goodwill ambassador since September 2000. She has traveled all over the world in this role, providing inspiration for others who want to help the world's children. Someone who has taken her message to heart is her son Ronan.

Ronan is aware that he has had many advantages, including an amazing intellect. He finished school at 11 and had graduated from college by the time he was 15. But instead of relying on this intelligence and his mother's fame to concentrate on making money, he has followed her example by joining the UNICEF team.

Ronan is a UNICEF spokesperson for youth. In December 2005, he joined his mother on a trip to Darfur, a region of Sudan that has suffered violence and severe hunger. He saw first hand the suffering of the 3.4 million people who had been forced from their homes.

"All across Darfur I talked to people and heard their stories, and of course I felt the pressing need to try to do something. There is a tremendous amount that the United States and people in the western world can do about Darfur," he reported. After returning to the United States, he wrote articles in several newspapers and added his voice to those who demand a lasting solution in Darfur.

Kids Helping Kids

Since 1950, kids in the United States have helped UNICEF by collecting money on Halloween while they are trick-or-treating. The tradition was started by five children in Philadelphia, Pennsylvania, who were concerned about kids in post-World War II Europe. They donated all the money they collected to UNICEF.

The next year, the Trick-or-Treat for UNICEF program started, and kids nationwide could be seen on Halloween carrying orange boxes and collecting change door-to-door. Since 1950, the program has raised more than $132 billion for UNICEF.

Gabriela Azurduy Arrieta, age 13, from Bolivia waits to speak while Audrey Cheynut, age 17, from Monaco addresses the UN special session on children on May 8, 2002. This was the first time children had addressed the General Assembly. The girls represented the Children's Forum of more than 400 boys and girls, which met before the special session.

WHAT DO YOU THINK?

Spread the Word
Which aspect of UNICEF's worldwide work do you think deserves to be better known? How could you let people learn more?

Voices of Youth

Today, it is hard to believe how the Internet once seemed exotic and unfamiliar. That was probably how people felt about it in 1995, when Voices of Youth—UNICEF's talking shop—began. In that year, UNICEF encouraged 3,000 young people to contact world leaders at the World Summit for Social Development in Copenhagen. The organization did not have a web site then, but Voices of Youth enabled young people to contact world leaders—and each other.

Since that time, Voices of Youth has developed as quickly as the Internet itself. Discussion boards, available in three languages, became known as the Meeting Place. Before long, young people were uploading messages, images, quizzes, and information about campaigns and children's rights.

Voices of Youth remains an exciting, interactive web site that gives UNICEF a real buzz. Like the Internet, it is constantly changing and evolving, but it maintains the three main features that give it special appeal. In these special areas, young people have the opportunity to explore, speak out, and take action.

Unite for Children/Unite Against AIDS

Children are the hidden victims of HIV/AIDS. UNICEF has understood this for years and has tried to make the rest of the world understand how much the disease affects children.

- Every day, more than 1,500 children under 15 are newly infected with HIV, mainly by their mothers.
- More than 6,000 young people between the ages of 15 and 24 are infected with HIV/AIDS every day.
- About 1,400 children under 15 die from HIV/AIDS-related causes every day.

Since 2005, UNICEF has sponsored a campaign to stop and reverse the spread of HIV/AIDS by 2015. This campaign is known as Unite for Children/Unite Against AIDS. The big difference between this and other campaigns is that it focuses on children. This focus should help the campaign concentrate on what are called the "four Ps":

- Prevent mother-to-child HIV transmission
- Provide pediatric treatment
- Prevent infection among adolescents and young people
- Protect and support children affected by AIDS

Glossary

advocate To press for change on behalf of others.

allies Individuals or countries who work together in a struggle. During World War II, the Allies were the countries (led by France, China, the UK, the U.S. and the Soviet Union) that opposed Germany, Japan, and their partners.

ambassador Someone who represents an organization or country.

civilian Someone who is not part of an armed force (an army, navy, or air force).

cluster leader A group or organization which gathers information to guide other groups in the area.

empower To give official power to.

HIV/AIDS HIV is an abbreviation for human immunodeficiency virus, which causes AIDS (acquired immune deficiency syndrome), a serious and often deadly disease. The virus is passed on in blood and sexual fluids.

immunize To help a person ward off an illness, usually through vaccination.

indigenous Describes people who lived in a country before those from other countries arrived there.

innovative New and imaginative.

jockey Someone who rides an animal, such as a horse, in a race.

land mine Buried bombs that explode when someone walks over them.

maternal Related to mothers.

millennium A year ending in 000; the most recent was 2000.

Model United Nations An event at which young people represent the countries and organizations of the United Nations.

mortality rate The number of people who die from a disease.

non-governmental organization (NGO) International organizations that are not part of any country's government.

nutrition The process of making sure people eat the right food.

pediatric Related to children.

penicillin An antibiotic medicine that helps fight infection.

poverty The state of being poor.

private sector (of businesses) Not part of a government; a business that aims to earn money for the owner.

psychologically Concerning the mind.

refugee Someone forced from his or her region or country because of war or natural disaster.

sub-Saharan Africa The part of Africa that lies south of the Sahara Desert.

sustainability Able to be continued without stopping.

tsunami A high, fast-moving wave caused by an earthquake under the ocean.

tuberculosis An easily-spread disease that attacks the lungs but also spreads through the body to the kidneys, spine and brain—sometimes leading to death.

vaccination Injecting a weak form of a disease into a person so that the body automatically builds a defense against all forms of the disease (including more dangerous ones).

World War I A war fought mainly in Europe between 1914 and 1918.

World War II A war waged around the world from 1939 to 1945 in which the Allies fought against Germany, Japan, and their partners.

Further Reading

Grahame, Deborah A. *UNICEF*. Milwaukee: World Almanac, 2004.

Maddocks, Steven. *UNICEF*. Chicago: Raintree, 2004.

Smith, Roger. *UNICEF and Other Human Rights Efforts*. Broomall, PA: Mason Crest, 2006.

Web Sites

http://www.gmfc.org/

The Web site of the Global Movement for Children, which is a worldwide movement of organizations and individuals sharing a goal—to unite to build a world fit for children.

http://www.unicefusa.org

UNICEF's United States Fund Web site provides updates on children in conflict-torn parts of the world.

http://www.unicef.org/voy/

Through UNICEF's Voices of Youth Web site, children around the world can participate in discussions and play games dealing with human rights.

http://uniteforchildren.org

This Web site provides information on how young people around the world are helping in the fight against AIDS.

Index